Published by Creative Education
123 South Broad Street, Mankato, Minnesota 56001
Creative Education is an imprint of The Creative Company

Art direction by Rita Marshall
Production design by The Design Lab

Photographs by AP/ Wide World (Stringer Yurikozyrev), Artemis Images
(ATD Group, Inc.), Gary J. Benson, Susan E. Benson, Steven J. Brown, Corbis
(Minnesota Historical Society), Anne Gordon, Bruce Leighty, Dennis Littler

Library of Congress Cataloging-in-Publication Data

Tiner, John Hudson, 1944–
Trains / by John Hudson Tiner.
p. cm. — (Let's investigate)
Summary: An overview of the history and uses of railroads.
ISBN 1-58341-260-3
1. Railroads—Juvenile literature. [1. Railroads.] I. Title. II. Series.
TF148 .T56   2003
385—dc21   2002034876

First edition

2 4 6 8 9 7 5 3 1

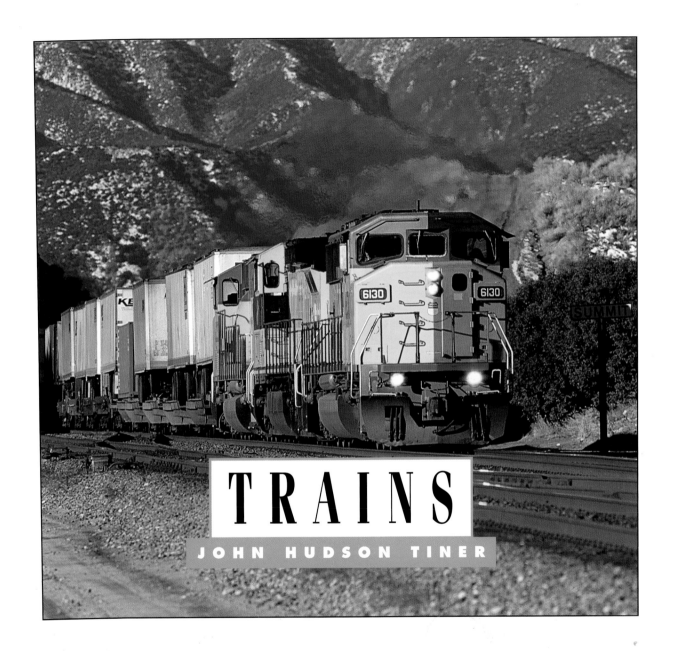

TRAINS

JOHN HUDSON TINER

Creative Education

TRAIN
ENGINEER

An engineer is a person who operates a locomotive. The engineer sets the speed with a throttle, sounds the horn as the train approaches road crossings, and operates the brakes.

Trains enable people to quickly move large loads over long distances

When the first trains began running along railroads in the early 1800s, many things changed. People's health improved because trains brought all kinds of fresh food from farms to cities before the food spoiled. People could travel quickly to the beach or the country for vacations. The vast American West was opened to settlement. In these and many other ways, trains changed the world.

TRAIN
FUEL

Both coal and wood were used as fuel for steam locomotives. In the United States in the 1800s, wood was the preferred fuel because of the abundance of trees.

TRAIN
POWER

*The first locomotives produced about 1.5 **horsepower**. The most powerful loco-motives today can generate 4,000 horsepower. Three locomotives may be put together to use 12,000 horse-power to pull a sin-gle long train.*

Locomotives must be powerful enough to pull many tons of cargo

THE FIRST TRAINS

A locomotive is an engine that pulls a train. Before trains had locomotives, they were called **trams**. Heavy railroad cars on metal rails were pushed by human muscle power or pulled by horses or mules. But even without a locomotive, cars that ran on rails were easier to move than carts on roadways. Wheels rolled more easily on the iron rails than on uneven and often muddy roads because the rails were harder and caused less **friction**.

Early locomotives had a cowcatcher—a metal, scoop-shaped grill—on the front to shove aside animals such as cows or bison.

A railway line is made up of three parts—railcars that hold the cargo, a railroad track on which the railcars run, and a locomotive that pulls the railcars. Scottish inventor James Watt built the first reliable steam engines in 1775. Inventors sought to propel trains with steam power rather than horses, but the first steam engines were too heavy and broke the rails. By 1804, steam locomotives were built with lighter engines and ran on stronger rails. But their top speed was only about four miles (6.4 km) per hour.

Above, a locomotive with cowcatcher Left, railroad tracks can be built almost anywhere

8

I n 1829, English businessmen hired an inventor named George Stephenson to build a 40-mile (64 km) railroad from Manchester, a large town filled with factories, to Liverpool, a port city from which goods were shipped around the world. The businessmen had planned to use horses to pull trams along the railroad, but Stephenson convinced them to test locomotives for the task. Four steam locomotives entered a contest, including one built by Stephenson and his son Robert. Thousands of people came to see the contest. The Stephensons' locomotive, the *Rocket*, reached a speed of 36 miles (58 km) per hour and easily beat its competitors.

Above, signal lights
Right, trains were
developed primarily
to deliver goods

he owners opened the Liverpool to Manchester railroad in 1830 with a big celebration. Steam locomotives hauled cargo between the two cities, but they also pulled **coaches** carrying passengers who enjoyed traveling at a faster speed than a horse could carry them. The era of train travel had begun.

TRAIN
ROUTE

The first railroad across the U.S. was completed in 1869 at the small town of Promontory, Utah. The last rail was hammered in place with a golden spike.

TRAIN
TIME

Time zones, *in which all cities within the same region keep the same time, were created because trains shared the same track. Accurate time-keeping became important to prevent trains from colliding.*

Railroad passenger lines sprang up quickly in the late 1800s in England and the U.S.

T R A I N
WEIGHT

*A train car fully
loaded with coal
weighs about 100
tons (91 t). A coal
train pulls about
100 cars, giving it
a total weight of
about 10,000 tons
(9,072 t).*

T R A I N
WARNING

*To prevent collisions
with trains at road
crossings, flashing
lights, sounding bells,
and a lowered barrier
warn automobile
drivers of approach-
ing trains.*

*A steam locomotive
creates steam (boiled
water) and smoke
(burned fuel)*

CHANGING THE WORLD

With the suc-
cess of the
train in
England, other coun-
tries—including the
United States—began
building steam locomo-
tives. In 1830, a small
American locomotive
called the *Tom Thumb*
raced a horse-drawn
tram. The steam locomo-
tive was in front for most
of the race until a
mechanical problem
caused it to fall behind.
Still, the *Tom Thumb*
proved that even a small
locomotive was more
effective than a tram
pulled by horses.

TRAIN
RECORD

The Trans-Siberian Railroad is the longest in the world. It stretches from Moscow in central Europe to Vladivostok on the Pacific Ocean, a distance of 5,778 miles (9,299 km).

TRAIN
FUNERAL

In 1865, a funeral train carried President Abraham Lincoln's body from Washington, D.C., to Springfield, Illinois. The last presidential funeral train was for President Dwight D. Eisenhower in 1969.

Workers laid and repaired thousands of miles of tracks in the 1800s

By 1850, most of the major cities along the east coast of the U.S. had been joined by 9,000 miles (14,480 km) of railroad track. By 1869, the first **transcontinental** railroad had been completed, and the U.S. had 50,000 miles (80,500 km) of railroad track.

TRAIN
TEETH

To climb steep mountains, trains are equipped with toothed gears (called cogs) on their wheels that fit into grooves on the track.

Above, the wheels of a locomotive Right, refrigerated railcars revolutionized food delivery

Trains changed lives, often in ways people did not expect. Trains brought perishable foods such as seafood and wild **game** to restaurants to be served fresh. They could deliver produce to market from farms 1,000 miles (1,600 km) away within 24 hours. People began eating a variety of foods and more fresh vegetables. Their health improved because of the better diet.

Trains also improved the speed of mail delivery. In 1838, England began sending mail by train. In 1863, mail railcars came into use. As the train sped along, clerks in the mail car sorted the mail. Small towns along the way hung their mail in bags along the track. As the speeding train came by, a hook snagged the bag and brought it aboard. At the same time, the mail clerks tossed the mailbag for that town into a net alongside the track.

TRAIN
NAMES

Trains are often given colorful names. The Puffing Billy *and* Tom Thumb *were two early trains. The* Flying Scotsman *was a 1930s passenger train, and the* Empire Builder *is an Amtrak passenger train of today.*

Above, an Amtrak passenger train
Left, trains have long assisted mail delivery

T R A I N
LEGEND

America's most famous train engineer was Casey Jones. He died in 1900 when his train, the Cannon Ball Express, collided with another train.

A passenger train bound for a wilderness vacation destination

In the late 1800s, railroad passenger companies in the U.S. tried to entice new customers to travel by train. They built railroads to an array of travel destinations and included the price of lodging in the ticket. Seashore resorts, hotels at Niagara Falls, and comfortable lodges at the Grand Canyon and Yellowstone National Park became popular vacation spots. People began to see train travel as a fun adventure.

PASSENGERS AND FREIGHT

Beginning in the 1860s, passengers traveling by train had three ticket choices. The most expensive fares were for first-class compartments, which were like small hotel rooms. Each compartment had a reading lamp, a table, a comfortable couch, and a restroom. At night, the passengers slept on fold-down beds. First-class passengers could order fancy meals in a dining car reserved for their use.

TRAIN
LUXURY

One of the best-known luxury passenger trains was the Orient Express, *which ran from 1883 to 1977 between Paris, France, and Istanbul, Turkey. It still carries passengers on special occasions.*

15

Passengers eating in a ritzy dining car in the early 1900s

TRAIN
TURN

When a high-speed passenger train is going around a turn, the railcars tilt to the inside of the turn so passengers are not thrown to one side.

An engineer controls a train's speed and operates its brakes

In second class, or coach, passengers enjoyed a comfortable ride with plenty of legroom, but they got no bed at night and shared the compartment with strangers. Third class was the cheapest fare of all. Third-class railcars were unheated, and often passengers had to sit on hard wooden benches. Passengers in second or third class could carry aboard their own food, or if the train stopped long enough, they could get off and order food at a restaurant. The **conductor** would tell them it was time to come back to the

Iron rails are held in place by large, nail-like spikes driven into crossties. The crossties, sometimes called sleepers or simply ties, are usually made of wood.

Above, rail spikes look like oversized nails Left, a freight train hauling grain

train by shouting, "All Aboard!" Today, most train lines offer first-class and coach-class tickets. Some countries, such as India, still sell third-class tickets, too.

Freight trains pull railcars that carry cargo rather than passengers. Freight trains transport goods such as coal, **ore**, grain, **livestock**, liquids, building materials such as bricks or lumber, and manufactured goods such as stoves or refrigerators. Freight trains are heavy and cannot go very fast. Their top speed is seldom more than 60 miles (97 km) per hour.

T R A I N
Y A R D S

Trains pulling railcars going to several different locations meet at a railroad freight yard. New trains are then put together with cars that are all going to the same place.

There are four basic types of freight cars: boxcars, flatcars, hopper cars, and tanker cars. Boxcars have sides and tops. They can be filled with boxes, barrels, or sacks of produce. A cattle car is a boxcar made with walls of wooden slats; spaces between the slats give fresh air to the animals being hauled. An automobile transporter is a special type of boxcar with three decks—one over the other—for hauling cars.

Hopper cars loaded with coal (top), and tanker cars filled with oil (bottom)

latcars have no sides or roofs. Large metal bins filled with cargo are often loaded onto flatcars. A locomotive pulls the flatcars and their containers to a location near the cargo's final destination. There, the containers are loaded onto trucks and hauled away.

Hopper cars carry loose raw material such as ore, grain, or coal. Hopper cars are filled from the top but have trap doors on the bottom to release the cargo at its destination. Tanker cars have large tanks filled with liquids such as oil, gasoline, syrup, or milk.

TRAIN
TANKS

The first train tanker cars used to haul milk were lined with glass. Today, milk tankers use stainless steel instead.

TRAIN
PASSING

When a fast train needs to pass a slower train on the same track, the slower train pulls off on a short section of railroad called a siding.

It is easy to load and unload stacks of lumber from flatcars

TRAIN
TREATMENT

Wooden ties are made of wood that has been treated with chemicals so it will not rot. A treated tie will stay in good condition for about 25 years.

Many cities today have train systems to lessen street and highway traffic

CITY TRAINS

In the 1840s, when trains often passed through large cities, railroads were built down the center of city streets. Because the trains had to share the streets with other traffic, traffic jams slowed them down. In 1863, an underground train system called a subway was built in London. The subway used a steam locomotive that spewed out smoke that fouled the air in the enclosed tunnel. Despite having to breathe in the smoky air, about 90,000 people rode the

London subway every day because it was so quick and convenient. Today, London's subway system carries almost three million passengers every day.

TRAIN
AUTOMATION

Some subway trains work automatically without an engineer running them. The trains stop at certain locations, and doors open and close automatically so people can get on and off.

TRAIN
SYSTEMS

Subway systems are known by different names in different cities. San Francisco has the BART (Bay Area Rapid Transit), London's system is called the Underground, and Paris has the Metro.

Some cities found that overhead railways were less expensive to build than subway tunnels. In the 1880s, New York City built railroad tracks up on stilts and ran trains above the city streets. Elevated trains avoided street traffic, but they created a loud clatter that bothered people living nearby. Because of the noise of elevated trains and the expense of building tunnels, some cities continued to use trolleys (carriages similar to trams) pulled by horses until the 1920s.

Chicago, Illinois, has a famous elevated train system called "the el"

Trains became quieter and less pollutive in the 1890s when electric motors replaced steam engines. Electricity reached the train by a third rail running down the middle of the track or from an overhead wire. The train collected the electricity by having a wheel run over the third rail or by a **boom** that reached up and made contact with the wire. New York City began running its first electric subway in 1904.

TRAIN
SOUND

A railroad rail is about 60 feet (18 m) long. A moving train makes a clickity-clack sound as the wheels hit the small gaps where two rails are joined.

Above, train rails Left, an electric train, with boom and wire overhead

TRAIN BRAKES

Before the invention of automatic brakes, trains carried a brakeman. He moved through the cars turning wheels on each car to put on the brakes and help stop the train.

24

Today, many major cities use trains to transport people from their homes to their places of work. These trains are called commuter trains. Some run at street level, while others are subways or elevated trains. Commuter trains reduce highway traffic and the pollution created by cars.

Below, a caboose
Right, a city's commuter trains may carry thousands of workers a day

ERIE

C177

TODAY AND TOMORROW

Toda... ...t trains are either fully electric or diesel-electric. A diesel engine ...... an automobile engine but uses a cheaper fuel called diesel. ...... engine aboard a diesel-electric train generates electricity to ....t turn the wheels of the locomotive.

Many trains, especially freight trains, burn diesel fuel for power

T R A I N

BULLETS

26

A modern electric passenger train in France, known as the TGV, can zoom along at a top speed of 238 miles (383 km) per hour. Germany, Japan, and other countries also have high-speed electric trains. Such trains can cover 600 miles (966 km) in about three hours. This is sometimes faster than the same trip by airplane because of delays at airports as passengers go through **security checkpoints**.

It's easy to see why this Japanese passenger train is called a bullet train

TRAIN
TEAMWORK

Diesel-electric locomotives can run with equal speed whether they face forward or backward. Sometimes two locomotives are put front to back and work together to pull a heavy train.

27

Above, a train pulled by three locomotives

TRAIN
WHEELS

Locomotives have large wheels that propel the train and smaller wheels that help support its weight. A 2-6-4 locomotive has two small wheels, six large wheels, and then four more small wheels.

Scientists are always looking for ways to make trains even faster. The friction of wheels on rails slows down trains. Smoother rails help, but another solution is to do away with rails entirely. Magnetic levitation (floating) trains follow a track called a guideway. **Electromagnets** are built into both the train and the guideway. Electromagnets push the train about one inch (2.5 cm) into the air and shove it along the guideway. A magnetic levitation, or maglev, train operated in Birmingham, England, between 1984 and 1995. In 1990,

In some cities, passengers can get around in fast-moving monorail trains

Germany built an experimental maglev train that traveled at a speed of 271 miles (436 km) per hour.

In the future, maglev trains may be enclosed in tubes that are filled with a light gas such as helium that offers less resistance to motion than air does. Passengers would ride in sealed cars with their own supply of air. Such a train might reach a speed of 500 miles (805 km) per hour and carry people or cargo from New York City to Los Angeles in about six hours.

TRAIN
RAIL

The iron rail used on tracks today is very heavy. A section six feet (1.8 m) long weighs about 300 pounds (136 kg).

TRAIN
TRACK

*Most rails are 56.5 inches (144 cm) apart. Narrow **gauge** rails are about 36 inches (91 cm) apart and make building a railroad easier in difficult locations such as mountains.*

TRAIN
TUNNEL

Trains can go under the English Channel through the Channel Tunnel, which is 31 miles (50 km) long. A trip from London to Paris, a distance of 279 miles (449 km), takes about three hours.

Whether carrying goods or passengers, trains make people's lives easier

For more than a century and a half, trains have been among the world's most important modes of transportation. They haul tons of cargo over long distances quickly and easily. They are a convenient means of getting around in large cities. And they offer passengers a cozy ride and a unique way to see the countryside. Trains changed the world, and they may again one day in the future.

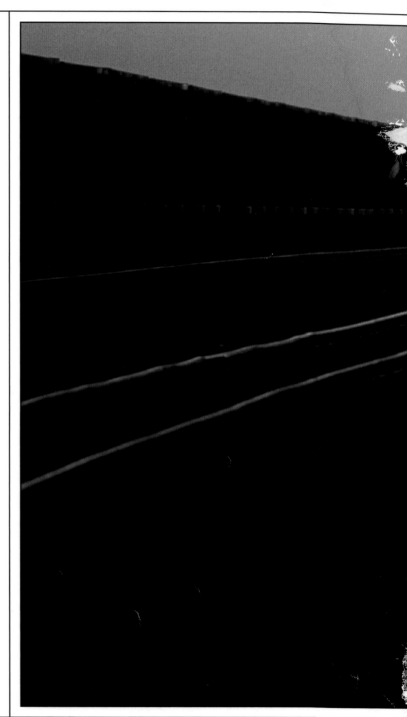

Glossary

A **boom** is a beam or pole that reaches out to touch a wire that transfers electricity.

Coaches are carriages that carry people; a railcar for passengers is sometimes called a coach.

A **conductor** is a worker on a passenger train who collects tickets and assists passengers.

Electromagnets are iron rods that become magnetic when electricity flows through them.

Friction is the force created when one surface rubs against another surface.

Game are wild animals such as fish, ducks, or deer that are hunted for food.

The distance between the two rails of a railroad track is the **gauge**.

Horsepower is a measurement of the speed at which an engine does work; a 1.0 horsepower engine can lift 55 pounds (25 kg) to a height of 10 feet (3 m) in one second.

Livestock are animals raised on a farm, such as cattle or horses.

Ore is a mineral (rock) from which a metal, such as gold or iron, can be removed.

Security checkpoints are places in an airport where passengers are checked for forbidden items such as weapons.

Earth is divided into 24 strips called **time zones**; every location within the same strip has the same time.

Railcars pulled by horses or mules were called **trams**.

A **transcontinental** railroad is one that goes all the way across a continent.

Index